snapshot•picture•library

HELICOPTERS

snapshot·picture·library

HELICOPTERS

FOG CITY PRESS

Published by Fog City Press,
a division of Weldon Owen Inc.
415 Jackson Street
San Francisco, CA 94111 USA
www.weldonowen.com

WELDON OWEN INC.
Group Publisher, Bonnier Publishing Group John Owen
President, CEO Terry Newell
Senior VP, International Sales Stuart Laurence
VP, Sales and New Business Development Amy Kaneko
VP, Publisher Roger Shaw
Executive Editor Elizabeth Dougherty
Assistant Editor Sarah Gurman
Associate Creative Director Kelly Booth
Senior Designer William Mack
Production Director Chris Hemesath
Production Manager Michelle Duggan
Color Manager Teri Bell

A WELDON OWEN PRODUCTION
© 2009 Weldon Owen Inc.

Library of Congress Control Number: 2009924570

ISBN: 978 1 74089 883 6

10 9 8 7 6 5 4 3 2 1
2009 2010 2011 2012

Printed by Tien Wah Press in Singapore.

A helicopter is an aircraft that has fast-spinning wings, called "rotor blades," on top and in back, that lift it into the air. Helicopters can fly up, down, forward, or even backward. They also have a special ability called "hovering," staying in the same spot in midair.

Helicopters can take off and land in very small spaces and at a moment's notice. This makes them perfect for all sorts of jobs. Police officers, firefighters, doctors, news reporters, and farmers all use them.

The main rotor
on top lifts the
helicopter up.
The tail rotor in
the back keeps
it flying straight.

The rotor blades in the back can be fully exposed or built into the tail like a fan (left).

Helicopters
can have bars
called "skids" or
wheels. Those
with floats can
land on water.

Helicopters are hard to fly.
Pilots use both hands and
feet to operate the controls.

Dials in the cockpit show
pilots information, such as
how high the helicopter is.

Helicopters take off
by flying straight
up into the air.

Once in the air, helicopters typically fly about 110–140 miles per hour.

Helicopters can stay still in midair. This is called "hovering."

If a helicopter is landing, don't get out or approach it until the rotor blades stop moving. As a rule, never go near the back of a helicopter—the rear rotor blades spin very fast and are hard to see.

Helicopters can do many different jobs because they can land in all kinds of places, like the beach.

Helicopters can fly across cities blocked with traffic, cross rivers, and reach islands quickly.

Some helicopters are used to
lift people from hard-to-reach
places, such as mountains.

Helicopters that work as air ambulances can reach accidents quickly and fly injured people to the hospital.

Others are used
for rescuing
people at sea.

Firefighters can scoop water
into buckets to drop onto
wildfires from helicopters.

Some suck
water up from
lakes and rivers
and carry it
in tanks to
fight fires.

The police use helicopters to help them fight crime.

Coast guard helicopters patrol
the seas, keeping people safe.
They also help in rescue missions.

The armed
forces operate
most of
the world's
helicopters.

Helicopters carry soldiers, equipment, and supplies.

The navy paints
helicopters gray.
This acts as
camouflage.

Hand signals guide
a helicopter pilot
to the landing
pad on the deck
of the ship.

Helicopters can speed reporters and cameras to the scene of big news events.

Helicopters can spray crops
with pesticide or fertilizers,
which is called "crop dusting."

Gyrocopters look like small helicopters. They are light and easy to fly, but cannot hover. Gyrocopters are flown for fun.

Helicopters take people to see
famous places, such as the Grand
Canyon or the Statue of Liberty.

Maybe one day you will climb onboard a helicopter and go for a ride.

Main rotor

A helicopter's main rotor has wings, called "rotor blades," that spin at a very high speed. This action lifts a helicopter off the ground and keeps it in the air.

Tail rotor

The tail rotor keeps a helicopter flying straight. Otherwise, it would spin in circles. It also controls which way the helicopter faces or turns.

Wheels

Some helicopters have wheels. These are useful on the ground for moving the helicopter into a hangar when the engine is shut down.

Skids

Most small helicopters have skids. These lightweight bars enable a helicopter to land safely on almost any kind of ground.

Floats

Some helicopters have floats for landing on water. These stop the helicopter from sinking and enable it to take off again from the water's surface.

Cockpit

The pilot sits in the cockpit and uses sticks and pedals to control the rotors. Dials track information, such as altitude. There's a radio for communication.

Search and rescue

Helicopters are used to find and rescue people lost in the mountains or other remote areas. If the helicopter cannot land, the crew can winch people to safety.

Air ambulance

Air ambulances are equipped to carry injured people to the hospital. They can reach accidents by flying over traffic and can rescue people where there are no roads.

Fire fighting

Firefighters use helicopters to drop water onto flames. They can scoop water from lakes or rivers into buckets. Some helicopters suck up water and carry it in tanks.

Police

Police use helicopters to monitor traffic, patrol large areas, and help in search-and-rescue efforts. They also use them to apprehend suspects and pursue stolen cars.

Crop dusting

"Crop dusting" refers to using aircraft to spray crops with pesticides or fertilizers. Tanks and spraying equipment are attached to the outside of helicopters.

Gyrocopter

Gyrocopters are built for fun. They fly at low altitudes, giving the pilot a good view of the surroundings. The speed record for a gyrocopter is 111.7 miles per hour.

ACKNOWLEDGMENTS

Weldon Owen would like to thank the staff at
Toucan Books Ltd, London, for their assistance
in the production of this book: Daniel Gilpin,
author and researcher; Ellen Dupont, project
editor; and Colin Woodman, designer.

CREDITS

Key t=top; b=bottom; af= age fotostock;
DT= Dreamstime; IA=Ian Armitage;
iSP=iStockphoto; P=Photolibrary
SST=Shutterstock; TP=Turbo photo
Jacket af; **inside flap** SST; **2** SST; **5** SST;
6 iSP; **8**t,b SST; **9** iSP; **10** SST; **11**t SST, b TP;
12t iSP, b DT; **13** DT; **14** iSP; **15** iSP; **16** IA;

17 DT; **18** SST; **20** SST; **21**t DT, b iSP; **22** iSP;
23t TP, b DT; **24** SST; **26**t DT, b iSP; **27** SST;
28t,b DT; **29** SST; **30** DT; **31** iSP; **32** SST;
33t,b SST; **34** SST; **36** SST; **37** SST; **38**t,b TP;
39 SST; **40** DT; **42** SST; **43** DT; **44** iSP; **45**t
DT, b TP; **46**t,b TP; **47** TP; **48** iSP; **49**t,b TP;
50 P; **52**t,b DT; **53** SST; **54** iSP; **55** iSP; **56** DT;
57t,b SST; **58** SST; **59** DT; **60** iSP; **64** SST.